Sleep

For Simon and Keturah with oodles of love, expert snoozers . . . now!

First U.S. edition 2019
First published by Old Barn Books (U.K.) 2018

Library of Congress Catalog Card Number pending
ISBN 978-1-5362-0798-9

TWP 24 23 22 21 20 19
10 9 8 7 6 5 4 3 2 1

Printed in Johor Bahru, Malaysia

This book was typeset in Times New Roman.
The illustrations were done in mixed media.

Candlewick Press
99 Dover Street
Somerville, Massachusetts 02144

visit us at www.candlewick.com

Sleep

How Nature Gets Its Rest

KATE PRENDERGAST

CANDLEWICK PRESS

Cats and dogs sleep curled up . . .

when they aren't playing.

Geese sleep at the pond,

chickens in the henhouse.

Horses sleep in the field

and cows in the barn.

Harvest mice sleep in their nests.

Snails sleep in their shells,

and so do tortoises.

Giraffes sleep
standing up.

Sloths sleep
upside down.

Bats do, too!

They sleep all day

and are awake at night.

Fish swim when they sleep
and never shut their eyes!

Meerkats sleep in a heap.

Penguins sleep in the cold.

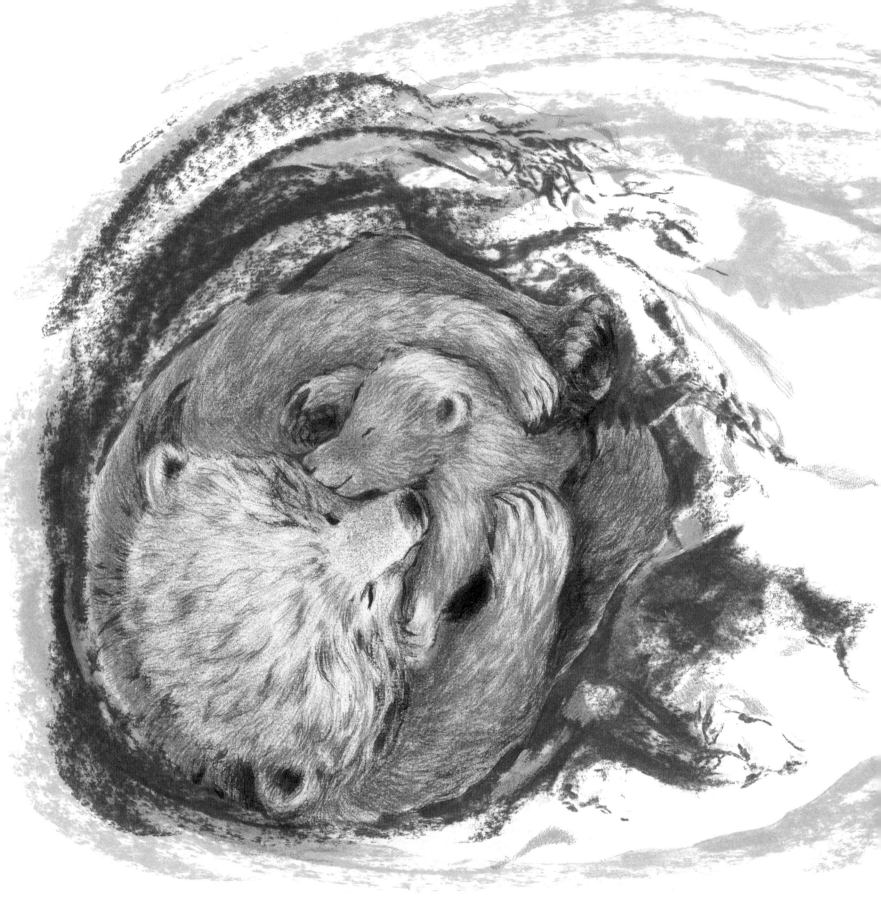

Bears sleep
all winter long,

but ants
sleep for
only a few
moments at
a time.

Every animal sleeps.

Do you think they dream?

How Do They Sleep?
A Closer Look . . .
and Some Other Fun Facts

Cats and Dogs

Cats and dogs sleep more than we do. Dogs sleep for twelve to fourteen hours a day, though often in short naps rather than one long sleep. Cats sometimes sleep for up to twenty hours a day.

Chickens

Farm chickens are descended from the red jungle fowl, which lives in the wild of Southeast Asia. Chickens like to sleep high up on perches, or in trees, where predators like foxes cannot reach them.

Horses

Baby horses, called foals, spend about half of their day sleeping until they are three months old. They lie down for their naps. As horses grow older, they sleep less and less and very often doze off standing up.

Cows

Cows lie down for up to fourteen hours a day. Like horses, adult cows sleep for just three to four hours out of every twenty-four, in naps of between one and five minutes at a time.

Harvest Mice

Harvest mice are active both during the day and at night, but they are most active at dusk. When a female harvest mouse is going to have babies, she climbs up a sturdy wheat or grass stalk and weaves a ball-like nest the size of an apple to keep her babies safe.

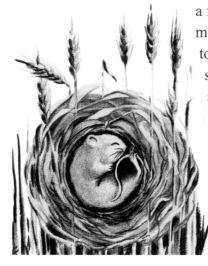

Tortoises

A group of tortoises is called a creep—not that you see one very often, as they mostly live alone. Tortoises' shells are made from the same material as fingernails and hooves. Most tortoises hibernate, going into a deep sleep for the winter months.

Giraffes

The giraffe is the
tallest animal on earth.
A group of giraffes is called
a tower. Although a giraffe's neck is very long,
it only has seven neck bones, called vertebrae,
the same number humans have. Giraffes
usually sleep for only thirty minutes a day.

Sloths

Sloths snooze for about fifteen
hours a day, high up in
tropical treetops. They
don't move very
much, but
they do
come down
from their
trees once
a week to
go to the
bathroom!

Bats

There are more
than nine hundred
different kinds of bats,
and they are
found almost
everywhere in
the world. They
sleep in caves,
or anywhere
dark and
cool—like
an attic—and
thousands or even millions of them
sometimes sleep together to keep warm.

Meerkats

A group of meerkats is called a mob. They live
in family groups of anywhere from twenty to
fifty. The mob sleeps in a heap, with the most
important female underneath the pile, and
sentries stay half-awake on the edge, listening
for danger.

Rhinos

Despite their bulky appearance, rhinos can run up to 35 miles/55 kilometers an hour! Rhinos have been around for 60 million years; their closest relatives are tapirs and horses.

Tigers

Tigers are the world's biggest cat. They can grow to almost 11 feet/3.3 meters long and weigh up to 660 pounds/300 kilograms. They are great swimmers and have been recorded swimming up to 9 miles/15 kilometers in open water. Tigers are an endangered species.

Penguins

Penguins never fall into a deep sleep, as they are always on the alert for predators. Instead, they take several short naps throughout the day. Emperor penguins can dive 1,600 feet/500 meters underwater and stay submerged for up to twenty minutes without taking a breath.

Bears

Bears hibernate, so when they wake up in the spring, they are hungry and hardly sleep at all. By the summer, they start to nap in the daytime, hunting only at night. Bears have the best sense of smell in the animal kingdom. They can smell seven times better than a bloodhound (whose nose is three hundred times better than a human's!).

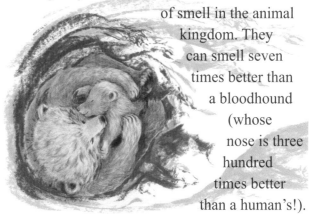

About the Author

Kate Prendergast loves to draw all animals, but particularly her rescue dog, Neo. While making this book, she was shocked to discover that so many of the wild animals featured in it are facing a conservation crisis and/or great pressure due to the destruction of their environment by humankind. She hopes that *Sleep* will help foster interest in the natural world and its protection.

Find Out More

Here are some websites where you can find out more about animal habits:

Animal Corner: **https://animalcorner.co.uk**

Mother Nature Network: **www.mnn.com**

National Geographic Kids: **https://kids.nationalgeographic.com**

Save the Rhino: **www.savetherhino.org**

The World Wildlife Fund: **www.worldwildlife.org**